D0722571

VENUS TRINES AT MIDNIGHT

VENUS TRINES AT MIDNIGHT

Astrological verses about Lions, Rams, Bulls, Twins, Archers, other Sun Signs, and you

Linda Goodman

Taplinger Publishing Company, New York

First published in the United States in 1970 by
TAPLINGER PUBLISHING CO., INC. New York, N. Y.

Published simultaneously in the Dominion of Canada by Burns & Mac-
Eachern Ltd., Ontario

ISBN–8008-7944-9

Library of Congress Catalog Card Number 75-108272

Printed in the United States of America

For Bill Webb
the skeptical Lion

who started it all with
a typical Leonine lecture
written in a letter dated
November 20th, 1968

". . . and so, you see, astrology is only one of several vocabularies, like music and art, that help us understand each other. But it's a singularly poetic language, with a unique expression for some of the rhythms in our lives. I want to learn more about it —not to become an astrologer—but to become a better poet. I like its sweep, its broad symbolisms, the fact that it's such an ancient old thing that hasn't changed for millennia. Poetry! Poetry! Poetry!"

my thanks to
the VIRGIN and the SAINT

Sheila Barry (Virgo) because she believed
Saint Subber (Aquarian) because he knew

also to the RAM
Dick Taplinger
because . . .

Contents

VENUS TRINES AT MIDNIGHT

Venus Trines at Midnight

Why do I fight sleep so hard?
        You're a fine one to ask, I must say

as if you didn't know
how I toss and turn in my bed each night
listening to the sheep dog snore
muffled sounds outside the door
a scream on the street that dies away
then far-off laughter

        The witching hour passes
        leaving the same, old, empty ache
        like a wisdom tooth
        with a cavity that needs filling

By two a.m. or so
the shadows seem to take form and shape
but nothing especially familiar

        Finally, I sink into sleep
        where you wait

           and it happens
           again and again and again
             three times

Then suddenly, angrily
I leap out of slumber

        to stay up till dawn
        reading and eating cinnamon toast

Look, something just has to be done
I refuse to have an affair with a ghost

Now that we're so intimately acquainted in dreams

for old times' sake

couldn't I run into your arms just once
when we're alone—and awake?

A Taurus Ascendant Is Sensual
but the Bull Is Conservative

I don't know why I bother to analyze him
That is, there are times you can run out of words
with some people
>   except for maybe "Good grief!"

For example:
>   He says he's glad that pot and nudism have
>   found us
>   "They provide valuable insight into the world
>   around us"
>   UNQUOTE (and there's more)

He walks alone by the ocean, collecting pieces of coral
and thinks Helen Gurley Brown is reasonably moral

>   (but he doesn't go much for drunks
>   or people who waste money)

He creates undeniably exquisite photography
though frequently I've heard him defend pornography

>   He develops naked women
>   in a dark room
>   with chemicals

Still,
he did make several very fine prints of an old tree
back in 1963

>   He hates the establishment with a violent passion
>   and he follows his dreams, after a fashion
>   Sometimes his conversation is esoteric and deep
>   but he doesn't believe
>   people astral travel in their sleep

and speaking of traveling
he takes a slow boat to China, by way of Japan
painting poetic symbols on an oriental fan
He digs Hopi philosophy—those Indians think he's great
and I can't deny he knows that "Kismet" means "Fate"

      Once I thought I saw him
      wearing a strand of love beads
      around his heart

But he can't even say "Om myoho rengay kiu"
to make a cab appear like magic, in the rain
or make a wish come true, by chanting it slowly
like any self-respecting flower child can do

      He's a phony, Victorian hippie
      shall I tell him?

Gemini—Gemini

I'm sorry I kept you waiting
Look, don't cry
it was only an hour or two
Couldn't you find something to do?

          I would have
       if I had been you

Jupiter Prayer on Christmas Eve

I'm in a panic

> the mistletoe and holly
> are tacked where they ought to be

and the wine is chilled

> but the ghost of Christmas last
> when December turned into a block of solid ice
> between us
> is leering through my shuttered window

You told me it was ghoulish to trim a dead tree
like hanging jewelry on a corpse in the parlor

> (Yours is naked throughout the merry season
> carefully tended in a pot of earth
> later planted outside where it can grow tall)

This year, mine is bare and potted too
and I give it lots of water

Yes, you'll like the tree

> it's the rug

that huge, spreading warmth
of the glossy, satin-brown Iceland Pony
on the floor

> I never thought . . .

> what should I do?

I can't hide it in the closet
It's jammed with other things that make you frown
my Frank Sinatra albums, all those ash trays
strings of colored lights and tinsel
and the poems I wrote last winter

>But I can't just leave it there
>I don't think I could stand the look on your face
>when you see that fur
>and the reflection in your eyes
>of the pony's pain when he was murdered
>>(or did he die a natural death?)

Never mind, it's still unkind
to have him stretched out on the floor
and walk across his beauty

>I hope it didn't hurt him—I really do
>and I hope it didn't hurt the steer you served me once
>at your house
>when he was struck in the head with a bloody axe
>by a butcher singing Noels
>with no ether

>>or the gentle, brown-eyed cow
>>who gave her life for your shoes

I find I'm crying now
for all of them

>>and I didn't want to cry again this Christmas

>There's the lobby buzzer
>you'll be at the door any minute

Oh, will you forgive me for the pony?

I won't walk across him anymore

I guess I know how that is . . .
like people you love
when they walk across your heart

      back and forth
      every day
      every night
      and think you have no feelings
      just because you lie there so still

Incantation of a Moon Child

Abracadabra rippled water tears
pickled pumpkin butterfly ears
north winds, blow across his years

I'll have my madcap moonlight way
no matter how many fiddlers call you
to a dance of wooden marchers

I'll leave my trace upon you
like a witch's hex
streaked through your hair
lingering in your silver eyes

I'll sear your palm with an eternal scar
so all the canny Cassandras will whisper

Ah, there goes one of the lost

he has been visited by a vagrant solitaire
singing a morning sonata
he has been wheedled by a will-o'-the-wisp
from the midnight moors
he has been kissed by a flickering firefly
brushed by the touch of a wild gypsy spell
he has heard the cry of a loon

he has been loved

Venus Exposed

Don't stand there
looking at me like that

> At least give me time
> to put on one of my masks
> There were seven false faces
> I brought along to this costume ball
> just to be safe
> but I seem to have mislaid them somewhere

Independence was stolen one stormy night last year
> while I watched you follow someone
> into a room
> and close the door behind you

Anger I haven't been able to wear
> since the day I hurt you with it

Pride I impulsively tossed out the window
> when I called
> to tell you I was sorry

Detachment, I guess, is permanently lost
> now that your smile
> brings a lump to my throat
> I can't swallow

Amusement disappeared without warning
> the morning I first knew
> what your eyes were asking

Frigidity melted forever
> the moment you touched me

Now, stripped of my protective cloak of poise
I toss my hair too often over my shoulder
tear napkins to shreds
order drinks I never finish
break match sticks into small pieces

What will I do to cover my trembling
when all my disguises are gone?

The only one left is Caution
and it almost flew out of my hands, just now
when I turned to go
and thought I heard you say

"Please stay"

Taurus

Is it you?

or is it just that I've made you wear those love robes
I've been saving
since the days when my sand castles
were big enough to walk around in
and strong enough to stand against the tides?

I can't remember who first said
that "what you don't know can't hurt you"
but whatshisname was wrong

Supposing I climb all the way to the top of the tree
and then find out

it's not really you

How do I get back down again
all by myself?

I've always been afraid of heights

Aquarian Awakening after Sundown

The skylark has stopped singing
from the roof of the Tin Pan Alley Record Shop on Broadway
if he ever was a skylark
I was never sure

and I don't reach out for your hand anymore
sometimes I stumble, without it
but at least I've kicked that habit of clutching air

How long has it been
since your arms were a rock of peace
to rest my head against

                three years already?

You passed by within inches of me this afternoon
while I was having a Hermit in the Muffinburger
                what did we used to say, as kids?

so near
"if he was a snake he would have bitten you"

Caught off guard
we looked at each other the way familiar strangers do
pulling the shades down quickly
over the transparent windows of our eyes
but not quite quickly enough
to hide the cluttered, broken dreams inside
like old furniture left behind
when love moves out suddenly

Your cool, casual nod
was almost a warning not to speak
so I didn't
It's just as well
What could I have said?
"How are you?"

I know how you are

You're sorry
and empty
and alone
like me

and it serves both of us right, I suppose
for being so proud and all

It's crazy, but I kind of thought you might call
after seeing you like that

I forgot
you can't
even if you wanted to

When you changed your number
I changed mine
and they're both unlisted now

Mars and Stars

Where is my shiny shriek blast
my breekle creekle fly sky high
my lyrical miracle
my spring ring fling
my crashing slappy flappy
Where is my happy?

Nothing is too good to be true
Nothing is too wonderful to happen
if you really want it to

I do
I do
I do

I know he didn't call
I know he didn't call *yet*

That's it—that's the word
yet!

Forever—forever
I'll never forget

that yet means imminent get

(according to both Webster and
God)

so . . .

rocket socket shiny shriek
and breekle creekle fleekle fast
my crashing slappy flappy happy
is not yet
but moon balloon soon and blast

The Fish Meets the Water Bearer

For Michel and Etienne
by any other Sun Sign, name or century

We searched for each other
in the most unlikely places
among the most unlikely people

and when our paths finally crossed
it was for reasons so entangled
in our daily bread
and the usual trespasses

that we might not even have noticed
except for that faint quiver of wonder
like a passing chill from the night air

        we loved

and the closest we've come to explaining why
is because it was you
and because it was I

Throw a Little Neptune In with the Image

I've learned a lot
from these last few political campaigns

> and if I ever try to make it
> as the first woman President
> running on the astrology ticket

the Mad Ave agency I want
is the one responsible for those Volkswagen ads

I always trust them
They start right out telling you their goofs
and how they fall a little behind a Rolls Royce

> but if I were running for the office
> of your wife, concubine, mistress, friend or pal
> I'm not so sure about that VW direct approach
> You can't use the same firm for private relations
> you use for public relations

I'd probably hire that other outfit
the one that makes you wonder
"Does she or doesn't she?"

> Then you wouldn't know
> if I do or I don't
> till I have

Pluto Moves Slowly but Surely

Look, my strawberry sometimes friend

Could I take a raincheck?

I'd like to skip this passing storm
with its violent thunder of knowing
between lightning flashes of guessing
and intermittent torrents of hurt

We're in that dangerous manic-depressive phase
of giving each other emotional ink blot tests
on public couches
and when one of us makes a Freudian slip
we switch roles
like two charming, but knife-sharp clever
diplomats
each unwilling to commit himself
for fear of an unexpected coup de grâce

Call me when it's time to surrender
my strawberry always love
I think I'll pass this next round
of Russian roulette with words

It would be just my luck to win

Linda Goodman

Title — Venus, Trine @
midnight; astrological
versus about
lion, ram, bull
twins, scales, +
other sun sign
+ you.

call # Ps 3557058444

The Aquarian Age of What

It was while I was having lunch today
at the next table
a man wearing one of those stick-on beards
and a yellow turtleneck sweater
was telling his friend

> "Do you know the *New York Times*
> just carried a story
> quoting top scientists and ecologists
> and they said that, in ten years
> this planet will be uninhabitable for humans?"

and the friend answered

> "Is that so? Well, let me tell you, buddy
> it's uninhabitable out where I live right now
> with all those blacks moving in closer
> and the neighborhood hippies
> with their damned motorcycles and
>   Peace posters
> and the liquor store down the street
> just lost its license
> so I've got to lug my booze home on the train"

and they laughed . . .

Later I checked it out
with the *Times* Information desk

> He was right
> that's what they said
> ten years

TEN YEARS?

> Doesn't anyone *care?*

I mean, ten years isn't very long
the years go by so fast these days

About ten years ago, Judy Garland was making a comeback
            no one had heard of Rod McKuen
            Butch Cassidy or the Sundance Kid
            there were three Kennedy brothers
            Dr. Spock was writing baby books

            Nixon told the press they wouldn't have him
            to pick on anymore
            and there wasn't a single tourist
            taking giant steps for mankind
            on the Moon

Ten years?

Has anyone told John Lindsay or Bess Myerson?
or Rap Brown
or Abbie Hoffman

or Howard Hughes?

            Of course, if *he* knew
            he wouldn't talk about it much, I guess
            he'd do something
            maybe he is . . .

but what if he's not?

                Ten years?
Does Charlotte Ford think about that
when she jets in her set?
I wonder if Richard Burton counted the depreciation value
when he bought Liz that diamond
Is that why Paul McCartney decided to split
then changed his mind—or did he?

Ten years?

Why, we haven't even discovered the cure for cancer yet
or figured out what to do with all that garbage
Do you suppose Ralph Nader reads the *Times?*

I have this feeling
I should send a telegram to the White House
but that's ridiculous
surely they have one of those clipping services . . .

> Would Abraham Lincoln or Theodore Roosevelt
> or Harry Truman
> have declared a national emergency?

I don't know—
"Give 'em hell, Harry"

> give *who* hell?

All the way home, my heart kept pounding in my chest
and I passed one of those signs in a window

SLEEP WITH A STRANGER TONIGHT

Well, yes, maybe—
maybe so
maybe fall in love with a stranger

> or with *someone*
> or with *something*—like life

Turn me on, dead man

TEN YEARS?

Capricorn Calendar

How old am I?
I'll be 92 next Christmas
though I won't admit to one day over 20

Even after all the birthday cards
are cut and shuffled
it's hard to figure

I've aged at least 500 years
since I stumbled into you
Yet I still believe in fairy tales
like "The Princess and the Frog"
    perhaps I'm really only 3 or so?

You'll never know how old I am
but I'll tell you anyway
I was born the hour we met
and died today

Combustible but Compatible

Because of that double sextile between our suns and moons
and all those Venus trines
it's hard to find a legitimate reason for a good healthy fight

       but we manage
       like last night

when we almost got caught in a storm
on our way to the new Japanese restaurant you found

       You said you didn't believe that junk
       about eggheads from Mars flying their saucers
       over our complacent chimneys
       I said maybe they could teach you how to park
       without leaving a space of four feet
       between the curb and the car
       I also mentioned how smug you are
       when you think you're right

Inside at the table, while you glared at your noodles
I lit my first cigarette in months
then you ordered yourself three rounds of drinks
and sat there through dinner like a stony Sphinx
When you wanted to leave
I wasn't ready to go
so I stirred my cold tea
for at least half an hour
watching you sputter
till you jammed your elbow down in the tofu
and smeared it all over your sleeve

It was spooky and silent between us
as we walked back to the car in a drizzle
and a fire truck tore by, with sirens shrieking

then suddenly we saw a squirrel
scurry up the trunk of an elm
and he looked just like the one we called "Charlie"
who ate from your hand
that weekend on Fire Island

      "He's a long way from home"
      you said
      we smiled at each other
      and after awhile it stopped raining

February People Are Real Pals

Lovers all use the same script
when they play their final scene

"Well, we almost made it, didn't we?
It's really better this way
I'll call you someday"
    after a love affair ends
    and they know it's time they parted

With you, it was
"Can't we be friends?"

      Friends?

That's how the whole thing started!

old chum, old pal, old Water Bearer buddy of mine
my comical, blundering, lost and lonely Valentine

Cancerian Cry

(CANCER CARES)

Those newspaper jokes
telling us how to celebrate
the national promotion campaigns
are getting pretty hairy

"It's National Pickle Week
take someone sour to lunch"

"It's National Agriculture Week
make out with a farmer's daughter"

"It's National Lamp Week
get lit up with your favorite lush"

"It's National Public Zoo Week
do the orangutang tango with an Ape"

How about "National Emptiness Week"?
rescue the lonely
they're everywhere
walking in and out of bars
with robot eyes that won't shut
till the street cleaners wash the city's dirty face at dawn

They sit around in all-night coffee shops
blinking in the purple-white neon light
dropping dimes into a slot
to dial a number that never answers

They stare at the deserted streets
from velvet-covered windows in penthouse prisons
and nurse a glass of lukewarm champagne, with no fizz
listening to the flashbacks of tired memory
stamped in the grooves of a record

Help the lonely celebrate
as they ride the subways
reading the newspaper upside down
	or stand in Nathan's
squeezing a plastic mustard container over a hot dog

	It's National Emptiness Week

		be kind to us

Venus in Virgo or Venus in Aries

People who learn passion from a book
the kind they mail in a plain wrapper
promising to teach you
where the erogenous zones are hidden
and all that other jazz

> can develop cardboard hearts and
> > paper emotions
> which fool some of the people all of the time
> and all of the people some of the time
> but not anyone real

Did you ever meet a champion
who learned the perfect timing of golf
from looking at pictures of Arnold Palmer
swinging a club?

Did you ever know a man
who learned the flowing motion of football
by reading about how Joe Namath does his thing
or even watching him pass the pigskin?

> I mean, love has a rhythm too

To look at pictures
of people reaching for the miracle of sex
is like learning grief
from watching Coretta King's face on television
or Ethel Kennedy's expression
as her youngest child moves restlessly
among the shadows on the lawn
> I look the other way
> I already know

My heart learned grief by diving naked
            into anguish
      long ago
            (though I've forgotten the exact day)

Maybe I've never dived so deeply
into that other urgent ocean of the soul
but I know this
People teach each other sex
and all those zones
if love was meant to be between them

            to learn the words and music
            of their own, alone and private song
                  together

So you read
            One Hundred and Sixty-Nine New Ways
            To Arouse Passion

and I'll read
            Lady Chatterley's Lover

What's wrong?
            Did you think I was going to say *Little Women?*

Scorpio Silence Is Golden

We'll never have enough of touching
after waiting so long
to do
and to be
what we want to each other

See how close we lie, in the slow, naked warmth
of our first morning of waking together
while our hands and our lips lazily practice
the intimate secrets they learned
in last night's sudden and violent surrender

even our toes
explore this strange country of total love
even our noses
the smell of your skin and your hair
is you, just you
so familiar
I would know you by that alone as surely
as I would know the scent of the woods we walked
from pine incense
or sherry from scotch

how quiet it is between us
our sleepy, sunrise kisses are not enough

now the strong circle of your arms tightens around me
                and I feel your need
till our new hunger is as fierce and as deep as before
then you ask silently—again
and I answer yes without words

I like this language
it's so honest
and simple
and pure

We've spoken it with our eyes since the beginning

Uranus in Libra Can Shake Up Mendelssohn

Come live with me

Marriage went out with Andy Hardy
and the Good Ship Lollipop
Not only that, it's a flop
just dig your parents, baby

When familiarity breeds contempt
we'll save the cost of lawyers
and those freaky courtroom scenes

whether we're richer or poorer

on some future, rainy day

Right now, the sun is shining
and anyway
a legal paper can't bind our hearts
or keep them from breaking
when one of us wants to go
or when one of us plays the fool

I'm sorry, I meant "if," not "when"
Don't lose your temper
Just count to ten
and keep it cool

By this time you should know
that the indecent show of a wedding
can't make you more my own than you are now

Come live with me
and share my bed
my modest wealth
my secret rituals

my sickness and my health

I may let you share my heart someday
Till then, I can teach you a lot
about the dynamics of a relationship
Like, two people who don't have a mystical bond
will run out of things to say to each other
and that's the end of the line
with or without a license to make a mistake

But two people who have loved each other for centuries
can never run out of emotional empathy
at least, not during one lifetime
and they make it through
without anything borrowed or anything blue

What do I mean by centuries?
Oh, wow—like, where have you been
Haven't you heard about reincarnation?
You're an atheist?
Well, nobody's perfect, so let's drop it, okay?
It's none of my business how you pray

The important thing is that sleeping together
won't change anything

        for better or for worse

Come live with me
Girl, I need you
don't worry about tomorrow
each day is sufficient unto itself
        (is that in the Bible or the Gita?)
Anyway, it's a good point to make to your mother
if she'll answer the phone when you call

Stop crying
I have a secret to tell you
you're not alone anymore

Say, listen, I hope you don't snore
and don't rap with me in the morning
that really drives me crackers

It's Not Easy to Please a Virgin

Since you grumbled your way into my life
with your Venus–in–Virgo slide rules and scales
and measuring sticks of perfection

I seldom get excited unduly
I'm on time for appointments
I can spell words like lapis lazuli
my stomach is flatter, I stand up taller
my ego is smaller
my hair is back to mouse brown
I've stopped smoking and eating bread
I go to bed earlier and wiser
I don't argue with rude waiters
get impatient with slow elevators
or knock people down in the street to grab the first taxi
            (well, not often)

But I still read Brenda Starr, Reporter
in the Sunday comics
wear pink goo on my lips
leave extravagant tips, when you're not looking
bite my nails now and then
sometimes forget to count to ten, before I speak
and last week
I had lunch in one of those plastic coffee shops

I'm sorry about falling a little short like that
It's just that I have to save some pieces of myself
in case I ever get bored
with being so beautiful and clever and good
and have to put the old me back together again

I hope that never happens
because this new me
is maybe the most me of me
I've ever known

As for you
to be absolutely honest, as you've carefully taught me to be
        you're still a little off-center
investigating truth, without consequences
        and doing your thing
playing with platitudes
reading books about Buddha
to learn how to die before you've started to live
straining emotions through a sterile sieve
and scrubbing your squeaky clean ivory tower
        with Brillo pads
each morning

      but you're improving

Three Galaxies—One

Isn't it wonderful that we have all that traffic at the corners?

> When we cross a street
> at an intersection
> and the cars streak by
> threatening sudden danger
> you reach out
> to grab my hand
> and hold it tightly

till we're safely on the other side

> Then you let go
> gently
> reluctantly
> not right away

Maybe that's why I always run against the light

> it's the only time we touch

Three Galaxies—Two

The odd-shaped things I save, that smell and feel of us . . .

>   a crumpled book of matches from the pizza place
>   some wilted flowers, picked outside the door
>   you couldn't enter

a bleached and crooked twig
washed ashore at that spot on the sand
where you first said you were lonely

>   and surprised me into tears

a hotel room key, stuffed inside an airline ticket envelope

>   a button you lost from your coat
>   (who sewed a new one on, I wonder?)

I guess you saved the bird verse
and the memory of my last smile
>   they take so little room in your scrapbook

Three Galaxies—Three

Most people love with restraint
as if they were someday to hate

We hated gently, carefully
as if we were someday to love

And now that you're gone
I'm free to cry at last
and to know
that I will be lonely for you
and you for me
through all the eternities before us

        but how much more so
        down here below
standing on the street where you left me

Don't Get Messed Up with a Fire Sign
if You Can't Stand the Heat

Darling
    (and I use the word tenderly
    though I often think you're a bore)

I'm far too fiercely possessive
and brimming over with impulsive dreams
to bring you any lasting peace

        I'd keep you up most nights till three
        just talking, or possibly walking beside the sea
        Then other nights
        I'd want to go to bed by seven
        to rediscover heaven

You could never count on me
to serve your toast and prunes on time
and every dollar you gave me to budget
would shrink quickly into a dime

        Floating around in a flowered mumu
        cleaning your castle
        with a broom and a mop and a dust rag
        just isn't my bag
        There are too many important things to do
        like breaking the chains that bind my hopes
        and one of those chains could be you

My heart flies free—not always wisely
yours has been carefully buried in frozen ground
    so it's really much better
        if we communicate with an occasional letter
        from Kalamazoo or Puget Sound

and I'll catch you the next time around

        Meanwhile, remember I love you

Listen, Shy Pussycat,
This Is Where It's At

(AT HALF PAST THREE TODAY)

So many things are curved and bent
twisted and pretzel-shaped
in our synchronized, schizophrenic relationship
I think we should try to unkink ourselves
before it's gone too far
which it probably has

> (you're already three hours late
> for our semi-annual date)

Let's get one fact straight
I didn't begin this charade in the shade
this game of freak-out croquet
this unpredictable roundelay
this put-on
this pure and remarkable friendship
upon which we're decidedly hung up
in this particular century

> You took me along to a three-ring circus
> and promised to buy me a pink balloon
> Then you tricked me inside the funny house
> with those crazy mirrors
> that made us look wavy and weird to each other

Not that I expected the scene
to be all cotton candy and thrills
or a strong man bending steel bars

> I just thought the stars
> might shine a little brighter
> from the top of the ferris wheel

but you've made them dimmer
and harder to see
since you stuck your Leonine paw in my popcorn

Before you climb back inside your cage
with the other superior animals
brace yourself, my proud and loopy Lion

you're wearing your smile upside down
like a lonely, haunted little boy clown
sadly riding a rigid merry-go-round
with no music in the calliope
no music at all

What's Your Moon Sign, Darling?

I asked him where he'd rather live
in an apartment or a home
and he grinned as he told me
    "A tree house"

Then I asked him how soon the moon would be new
to wish on
but he sighed when he answered
    "Maybe three days from forever
    or very possibly never"

Tonight we were watching our first fire together
when he laughed and pointed

    "See there?
    the flames look like a horse—with six legs
    Wonder how fast he could run?
    If I knew his name
    I'd make a two-dollar bet
    and buy you that wish when I won"

Once I saw him paint a turtle
He used emerald green, snow white and bright yellow
yet his moods are frequently brown
The thing is, you see
he's a poet
who never bothers to write it down

Premature Gotterdammerung

I have pondered long and sadly
what you said
about the certain, tragic future just ahead
for a waning planet, drenched in murky, poisoned air
infected by polluted oceans, swollen with rancid refuse
nature's cool green velvet quilts
ripped and ruined

land laid waste and ravaged
bleeding from the rape of greedy gorging
stripped naked of its nourishment
by blind and selfish plunder
haunted by the shrieks of murdered baby seals
and the ghosts of butchered leopards

soaked through with the stench of sure decay
the final gasp so near
it must be measured by the year
instead of by the century

and so, you say, you will not bring a child
into a world so soon to be expired

I've shuddered at the harsh statistics of despair
which could allow this sterile judgment
to find roots in such as you
whose tears reflect the memory of angels running free
through fields streaked yellow by the morning sun
whose ears still hear the carols of their laughter

And, as always
I have rushed to walk beside you on your way to truth
to try to see it clearly through your eyes

You paint a picture of a lovely, pulsing ball

within our solar system
profanely debauched by amoral brutes
who have used it shamefully, for pleasure
and torn its flesh
with repeated, painful nuclear thrust
to father grotesque mutation

who have bruised its fragile beauty
leaving it to die
like a frail, emaciated body
pale and wan
while they lie drunk and babbling senseless songs
"Diddle Diddle Dumpling, My Son John"
going—going—very soon gone
slain in careless orgy
just before the dawn
of hell

And now I feel with you excruciating sorrow
and share your angry, urgent need
to halt this mad and ruthless blasphemy
that threatens man and beast and fish and fowl

We can, we shall, we must
pull back these lengthening shadows from our sun
and mobilize each outraged soul
to strike a furious blow for life
        today
before tomorrow's lost in dust
Don't stop to count the cost in time or coin
when it may be too late
before another dozen springs of ours
        or theirs
have passed

        But wait—
listen to the soft, permissive sighing

as erotic lullabies of doom
crooned to lazy, silken melodies
are amplified through spinning, electronic discs
and whirls of flashing, colored lights

Look closely in the burning face of evil

Unholy masquerader—
who is that
who gazes back into our eyes
with smile so bright
his hair so fair and golden?

Who is that
who sits so tall behind the wheel
to press the gas
and vomit fumes of filth into already sickly air?
Who dares to multiply himself into a hundred thousand devils
swinging in a frantic, frenzied dance of death
dumping trash in the streams of Michigan
to keep Ohio clean?

Burst a bag of shiny dreams
see how white the toothpaste gleams?
Break it, smash it, spit out cans, stain the sands

Who dares explode hydrogen hate
deep inside the bowels of earth
stirring sleeping giants
to stretch awake beneath the soil, unseen?

Who hides behind screaming banners of progress
bulldozing flowered meadows, slashing trees
clubbing wildlife, grabbing pasture, faster—faster
plaster billboards, spread cement
for countless millions of polished beetles
blasting down the midnight roads

groaning under loads of drugged and singing
saints of sin?

Who dares excite the fire that lights the fuse
on the time bomb of a billion random seeds
sprung from the sensual loins of lust
adding wanton procreation to destruction

Who is curious, yellow, for topless, bottomless, mindless sex?
Are not insane, lewd scenes of human violation
as much a crime
as those against *her* pure and spacious skies?
She, remember, also once a virgin
proud of purple mountain majesties
and amber waves of grain

Look fiercely in the face of evil
see how he wears a crown of crimson roses on his head
to greet the newly wed
and nearly dead
on their journey into nothing

How dare he imitate your blameless, honest features?
How dare he call with carefree voice to sound like mine?

Look hard into the glittering eyes of evil
be sure you see

              his face is you—his face is me

belching blindly in the market place

Call the vile and vicious stranger in our midst
by his rightful name, with shame

              for only then
will truth come crashing through the constellations
              in time to turn the tide

                    and only then
can we make fresh clean winds blow once again
across the snowy mountain tops of this dying earth

                    and only then
deserve to hear his waiting, newborn cry
wrapped in the gentle blankets of our longing
                    and our love

Mercury Survival Kit

If you ever get caught in a round or two
of the head shrinkers' current favorite game
called "truth confrontation"
prepare yourself for a possible shock
that can lock a heart
or screw a mind uptight

You know the rules
All players sock it to each other like it is
to peel away layers of self pretense
with no points given
for the desperate maneuvers of self defense
or strategies to salvage pride
        and when you pass "Go"
        you collect 200 pieces
        of a massive wounded ego

But if you really want to win
and cut straight through all the lies
remember that you don't play "truth" with words
you play it with your eyes

Cancer Ruling the 4th House

I don't suppose I know you well enough to tell you this
(it's very intimate and personal)

> but there was this house on 8th Street
> in Parkersburg, West Virginia
> where my grandparents lived

and there was a rope swing, with a board to sit on
upstairs on the back porch, just off the big bedroom

> > I used to swing there for hours and hours
> > and think the most fantastic things
> > Once I swung all the way to Japan
> > and didn't get back in time for supper

Then there was this chest, in the attic
with so many marvelous mysteries inside
scraps of lace from ball gowns
covered with shimmering mother-of-pearl sequins
a white nurse's veil with a bright red cross on the front
faded, yellowish kid gloves, soft as whipped cream
and my aunt Peg's wedding veil, trimmed with
> > tiny orange blossoms
smelling like cedar
I used to wear it and pretend I was a bride

(That's as close as I ever got to that dream
> Oh, I got married, all right
but I was never a bride with a veil in a church)

> > The most important thing about that house
> was the crystal chandelier, with hundreds of
> > sparkling prisms
> hiding the infinite multiplication of the spectrum

It hung over the oval table
in the dining room downstairs
and every Saturday afternoon
        (it had to be a sunny day—rain spoiled it)
I stretched a cord across the huge bay window
that looked out on the rose bushes and the bird bath

            and I hung the prisms on the cord
            one by one
            and when I finished
            the sun shone through the crystals insanely
            till every corner of that cozy room
            was splashed with dancing rainbows

thousands and thousands and *thousands* of rainbows!
        Isn't that simply fabulous?

I guess I don't know you well enough
I told you it was intimate and personal

Alice's Hexagram

In the beginning
I used to puzzle myself
about what was missing from our Wonderland

> (certainly not the Red Queen or the Mad Hatter
> it was only yesterday that we had tea with them)

and after I knew what it was
our moments together were smudged with restlessness

> but now I sit near you
> quietly content
> and deeply peaceful
> gazing through the looking glass
> of a car, a bus, a plane or a train
> paying no attention at all to the White Rabbit
> and his threatening pocket watch
> nor to the second hand

For I Ching says:

> when the clouds grow heavy with moisture
> one only has to wait
> the rain will surely come
> ten pairs of tortoises cannot prevent it
> and perseverance furthers

California Squares and Sextiles

Look back again

to San Francisco's cable cars, climbing flowered paths

> to Hollywood and Vine
> Big Sur and Tiny Tim
> the Christmas one, with crutches
> and the one who tiptoes through the tulips

Look back

beyond the foaming, troubled surf
to where you left your heart
along the winding roads that lead from Carmel to Nepenthe
Look back to pine trees, reaching up toward tomorrow
and the ones with palm leaves drooping in the smoggy air
near MGM and Paramount

> It's not too late

Look back

at Jaguars speeding past the dreamers
sipping lemon cokes at Schwab's
a lone, white cross planted on Mount Olympus
against the far hill
behind Grauman's Chinese Theatre
and the signatures of gods and goddesses
graven in cement, below

Look back once more

> at the golden stretch of beach called Malibu
> where Jess Stearn writes away the hours
> haunted, maybe
> by the echoes of a sleeping prophet

Sunset Boulevard at sunrise
blurring streaks of colored neon on the Strip
waving in zigzag patterns through slanting veils of rain

the train, at L.A. depot
spilling passengers afraid to fly

Listen to the throbbing "Sounds of Silence"
and the whimpering cry of Rosemary's baby

Clap your hands for Tinker Bell
and sigh for Peter Pan
frolicking among the dancing fountains
and jungle blooms
of the Beverly Hills Hotel

Stop beside the gateway guarding garish Forest Lawn
long enough to wonder what twilight has to say
that she should linger on this way

Look back

at lonesome cowboys and girls in scarlet tights
swinging on a high trapeze with bearded Lancelots
and barefoot priests of fantasy
from the other side of the grass
—where it may be greener
as Dustin Hoffman challenges John Wayne
to a duel in the sun

Look back again
at the uneasy ground where San Andreas lies at fault

but blameless

driven near to breaking by something more than nature
bombarding every inch of earth around its bed

It's not too late
Look back

at Woodstock's lavender smoke
winging magical mystery signals to Paul and John and Mark
and others in the endless line of children
walking through the loneliness with lighted candles
chanting "Peace"

and crying out against a hundred kinds of hate and greed
and war

sending strong, electric waves of love
to the trembling Pacific shore

My God! You didn't see them?

They passed right by your door

Aries Is Aries

Our first argument was over music
for want of a better excuse

　　　The recording was instrumental

first the Mars crescendo, pounding, pulsing, thrilling, wild
then the Venus passage, gentle, feathery, delicate
like the daydreams of a child

　　　contrast marked

You started it, not me

　　　You said, "That Mars type music turns me off
　　　It grates on my nerves like Aries people
　　　who fly too high
　　　All it's good for is a battle cry"

The challenge was sharp and unexpected
but I felt an instant flame rise up to meet the danger

"You're wrong!
it's alive and strong and real
It's exciting and it's honest
and somehow, it makes me feel . . ."

　　　"Aggressive?" you asked
　　　with the curious smile of a stranger

Your casual detachment was worse than anger

　　　"Don't be so tense—
　　　now listen to Venus
　　　It's peaceful
　　　and soothing
　　　and tranquil . . ."

"And boring," I finished
"like someone who can't find the courage to weep
It puts me to sleep"

  Silence
  then —

"Mars doesn't have to mean war," I ventured
"it's just that it's brave and true . . ."

"And forceful and driving," you interrupted
and terribly exhausting, like you"

  It cut deep
  and left a few minor scars
   (not that they'll ever show)
  Later you said you were teasing
   "I'm sorry"

You're a cool, clever liar, you know

So, for weeks I've been troubled and chastened, I guess
and slightly ashamed of me
I had almost decided to put Mars on the shelf
and make milky soft Venus a part of myself

  But today is Thanksgiving
  with the Macy's parade
  just outside my window

and the drums are beating, frantic and loud
while my heart leaps in tempo with the roar of the crowd
Yes, it's true that's the music they play at the front
to make men brave

All right, war is murder—I hate it as much as you
but I didn't invent it—can I prevent it?
And even if I try
what's wrong with being brave enough to die?

I can hear your answer
"It depends on *why*"

Oh, God, must semantics be part of our season?

You may give me a reason to need my Mars someday
So, if it's all the same to you
I haven't thrown it away

Moon in Libra, Growing Old Gracefully

When I think of you

    I don't need the crutch of cigarettes or coffee
    to face the morning

When I remember you

    I scold the dogs more gently if they climb upon my bed
    against the rules

Because of you

    I buy a bunch of violets every Tuesday
    when they're in season
    and bring them home, and keep them till they wither
    for no particular reason
    except that once I saw them sleeping
    near a bristlecone pine in Cripple Creek, Colorado

Since knowing you

    I haven't felt it necessary
    to win each game of chess I play
    I notice lonely people more
    on holidays—like Christmas
    place fewer ornaments upon the tree
    I like things naked
    even me
I'm more compassionate and patient with fools who bore me
even with the ones who ignore me

I take long walks
and yesterday I bought some colored chalks
to try to make a picture of a child

Yet, I can't find any mention of this magic
in the songs of Solomon
the sonnets of Shakespeare

Montaigne's essays
or Walter Benton's poems

They wrote of friends
or lovers
who come together now and then
We haven't said hello since August
or was it June?
that rainy evening—
or was it late afternoon?

We cannot call this love
How could it be
when we've never touched each other
and perhaps we never will
when we have only come as close
as resting elbows on a sill
and looking through the windows of an empty house
listening to the droning buzz of bees
kissing tangled clouds of baby's breath
and blue forget-me-nots
growing near a broken picket fence

as children do, in enchanted gardens
they half believe are haunted

Nor can we call this friendship
Friends share tragedies and joy by telephone or letter
Our last communication was a postcard in July
Why, one of us could even die
without the other knowing
in time to send some flowers to the church
or light a candle at a distance

It's like you told me once
if we never saw each other again
it wouldn't make any difference

you didn't say it wouldn't matter
you said it wouldn't make any difference

and did you know I understood the nuance?
It was so long ago
but, did you know?

Any Planet in Gemini Can Be Deceptive

(BUT USUALLY THEY JUST LIE TO THEMSELVES)

Yesterday, I got a six-page, single-spaced letter
from a Gemini type

> (which is uncommon enough in itself)

I believe it was on page three, he wrote

> "As for me
> everything I do
> I do with everything I've got"

I wonder, should I allow him to cling to his Mercury myth?
Or shall I remind him of that morning in San Francisco
near noon
when the sun was hot and the waves were lapping
and it was time to leave too soon

I distinctly remember the obvious blending
of his heart and his mind and his soul

> but his body was not there at all
>   (or maybe just under incredible control?)

No matter, my point is made
It's just not true, Mister Magoo
although you do a lot

> you do not always
> do everything you do
> with everything you've got

Riddle of October 25th, 1969

Jennie Rebecca Goldman
grabbed the center of the stage
at a very early age
when Barbra Streisand sang a song
about the joys and sorrows of all her tomorrows

What else can you expect
of a fiery Mars-ruled Aries girl of three
timidity?

Now she's nearly eight
and still a child of fate
for last night, very late
as she lay dreaming of winning each game
a strange, laughing man from her own native planet
     (maybe Victor was his name)
slipped through her nursery window
and whispered a secret to guide her
something to hold forever inside her

After tucking her in bed
and turning out the light
Jennie's mother heard her cry

    "I just saw Venus in the sky!"

Happy, happy, happy future birthdays
Jennie Rebecca Goldman
and Merry Christmas too

    though you're standing in the sunlight
    keep your eyes upon the stars
    at the hour you saw that wondrous sight
    the Moon was in the Seventh House
    and Jupiter aligned with Mars

Your sister Suzanne was there with you
she saw it too
and across the town
when a six-year old named Mark lay down
to watch the planets' mysterious pattern
he called through the dark, at the very same time

"Oh, mother! Come look at the rings around Saturn!"

Your Moon Conjuncts My Mars in Gemini

If they recognized champions

      in the field of non sequiturs

like they do in baseball

      (May the Brooklyn Dodgers rest in peace)

Your name
would long ago have been emblazoned in the Hall of Fame
of verbal dexterity immortals

      for outstanding achievements like

"No, it hasn't happened between us yet
and it never will—so far"

      I truly consider that one of your finest efforts
      not to communicate the lie
      of the truth you didn't say
      Touché?

Venusian Vibrations

Will someone please tell Hilly Elkins
who thinks those couples prancing around nude
      in *Oh! Calcutta!*
are the last word in throbbing, sensual passion

      that yesterday I saw two people
      sitting across from each other
      in a crowded, noisy coffee shop
      holding eyes and touching hearts
        and knowing
      how soon and how deep
        but waiting
        just a little while longer

in case he ever wants to produce a show about sex?

Pluto in Cancer, Exploding

You want to take a trip
or at least blow a little grass
and you need to borrow some bread?

Sorry, sweetheart—I would if I could
your credit is good
it's just that I'm low on cash
and the little I've got
won't buy any pot
let alone acid or hash
It's really a pity, but I'm strictly "tap city"

Don't go—I'll walk with you awhile, if you want me
and show you what it's like to be born and to die
in one moment of time
I mean, like my own kind of hegira

Look just behind your shoulder
there's a tall, thin steeple
drawing a needle shadow to thread all the people

> See the fat lady, winking at the clown
> running up the steps where the lions lie stoned
> guarding the courthouse door?

Cars on the left—cars on the right
go-go-go on the green-green light
stop on the color of raspberry jello
The sun is so bright
it's kind of like drowning in brilliant orangy-yellow

> I know a place with quiet cool shade
> where we can walk barefoot
> and chew pine needles
> to make it Christmas

80

Here in the woods, it's dark and deep
like sleep
we can whisper
and no one can see us or hear us
but God
and He's smiling

        Now come over here
        lie down—touch me
        feel the grass
        it's green and wet and new
        no, not with dew
        Those sparkling drops are diamonds
        and part of the wet is me and you

Your eyes are bursting with colors
and twinkling lights and star shine
they're reflecting the Queen Anne's lace by the pool
        and speaking of royalty

do you know you remind me so of King Arthur?
There's still the faintest scar on your forehead
from the wound when you were searching for the Holy Grail

        but listen

do you hear all that love pouring out of the sky
like music?
what a glorious, bell-ringing sound!
it could really blow your mind
whipping in and out of the breeze that's tangling your hair

        Hey, doesn't the air
        smell like vanilla?

It's such a fiercely gorgeous high
are you sure you want to smother it?

Your Horoscope Shows a Talent for Music

"Personally, I think there's a lot to be said
for the Jungian theory of synchronicity"
                    (Prelude in a minor key)

"Say, did I ever tell you
about the time I went camping with some Indians
and got high on peyote?"
                    (Improvised jazz)

"Over tipping is demeaning, you know
Ten percent of the bill is plenty"
                    (Broken rhythm)

"I almost joined a nudist camp last summer
but then I thought of that god-damned volley ball"
                    (Melody played in G flat)

"What takes you so long to get dressed?
Aren't you ever on time?
We'll be late again—but you look beautiful"
                    (Chord progressions)

"Don't worry about the past
tomorrow's another day
I'll meet you next week in Santa Fe"
                    (Symphony, symphony, symphony)

Air Sign Rejected

Before you leave

> give me your hand again, for just one foolish moment

> I'll race you to the moon!
> The cold night wind will blow the cobwebs from
>   your soul
> and I promise we'll be back by noon

Ah, but wait
It's much to late for you to race through space

> This you tell me with the sad and empty eyes
> of one who knows the moon's too far away
> to reach in just a day
> let alone within the hour you can spare

All right, no flight tonight
Tomorrow—back to yesterday

> "Do you want a round trip ticket, sir?"

> "No. I'm just going one way"

Follow That Star in the East, Officer

Were you there at the miracle of Woodstock?

the third largest city in New York State
surrounded by tiny rivers of hate
conceived in magic
born in music
and rocked in fields of alfalfa, baby

Were you there on the highway called Happy?

where the Jefferson Airplane streaked through the sky
explodin' like a comet over Philippine Pond
while the cattle were lowin' and roamin' around
diggin' the sound
and the Wise Men rode on a Day-Glo bus

"Oh, come along with us
and make the scene
where Groovy Way meets Gentle Path
at the intersection of Freedom
and we'll all take a bath in milk and honey

Come along now
and we'll reach for a song
we'll drink up a cupful of green meadow grass
or some rain on the rocks
and we'll find us a bed near the Grateful Dead

Girl, if you go, I'll tell you true
the road's not straight

but just you wait
till you see the view
from the top of yourself

Were you there at the miracle of Woodstock?
where the hazy smoke of Uranus dreams
softened the cries
of Melanie by the Mountain
Did you drown with Joan in cool Sweetwater
to the piper's patter of Blood, Sweat and Tears

Were you there?
did you care
when Arlo jumped clear over the Moon?

Hey, diddle diddle, that cat and his fiddle
He turned on the stars not a wish too soon

Did you see the horizons of multitudes?
wearin' rainbow robes and muddy boots
where Country Joe shared his Fish in the stable
with a couple of loaves from Max's Farm
and Man, it poured down all that bread
on all those beautiful people
like it did before
way up in the hills
when everybody shared his picnic basket
at that great Jerusalem love-in

Oh, were you there when we rang the bells
     of Woodstock?
so Richie Havens could hear us pray
while Janis flew high on the Milky Way
How long did she stay out there and groove?

Girl, did you throb
to the chant of love me
touch me—heal me
feel me turn to gold
beneath soggy tents of plenty?

Oh, girl, did you feel me turn to gold?
Then let it be told
that the sermon was preached with Creedence
at that swingin' Clearwater Revival—so fine
in the Year of our Lord
Nineteen hundred and sixty nine

Did you catch the sight of Jimi and Tim?
takin' up a collection of warm
while the choir sang true
with an Incredible String Band
that wrapped your head in swaddling blankets

      Were you there at the miracle of Woodstock?
where the Canned Heat burned
around the Butterfield Blues
eggin' on the Quill to call Santana
and spill more chords on Sly
so the Family Stone could pass the laughter
for Ten Years After

      How many Bulls kissed a Moon Child's eyes
      near the tree
      where the Ram lay down with the Lion
      and the Goat learned to talk with the Virgin
to the echo of a hundred guitars
and the Twins touched Venus on the way to Mars

      Were you there with the many
when they saw the Who?
Did it tremble you
to hear Johnny Winter come wailin' through
a summer sky
tossin' midnight moods to Bert and Ravi
Did you wonder why it made you cry?

Oh, how many ballads do you think were sung
by Keef and McDonald
for the love of Crosby, Stills, Nash and Young
and how many babies were bundled in sighs
to the rhythm of Sebastian's rock-a-byes
cradled by The Band that filled this big land
of the rocket's red glare
with LOVE burstin' in air
to give proof through the night
and by dawn's early light
that the message was there

so far out of sight
it left your mind
way behind
your soul

Were you there at the miracle of Woodstock?
when five hundred thousand Aquarian hearts
whispered a secret from one to another

"There's a lot of us here
and if we're all gonna make it
we'd better remember
each guy is our brother"

so

Peace, Man, Peace

oh, tidings of great joy!

oh

Peace, Man, Peace

If My Calculations Are Right . . .

Without a crystal ball or ouija board
I can't be sure what's going to happen
            tomorrow
next week, next month or next year

just the astrological vibrations
of the negative-positive cycles
            are clear

        but I know exactly what's going to happen to me
        on Christmas Day, October 25th, 1993

I'll run slowly into Central Park
to smell the Gingko trees
and find you walking on a bench
feeding the squirrels Limburger cheese
and playing marbles with jelly beans

        The corners of your eyes will have a few
            more crinkles
        mine will too
        and some of our dreams will have a few
            more wrinkles
        from not coming true

You'll be munching a slice of blueberry pie
and of course your white horse will be somewhere nearby
                (the one you always ride
                when you're chasing lost causes
                through the skeptical sky)

I'll murmur
    "Fancy meeting you in Never-Never Land"
When you hold out your heart, I'll hold out my hand

and at that very same moment
a church bell will chime

      (like the one we heard
      that snowy Sunday morning in New Haven)

Then birds will swim backwards
and fish will fly high
frogs will sing love songs
and I'll start to cry

      when I hear you smile
      and see you say

"Remember? I told you we'd find a purple leprechaun
to wish on someday"

Three Lions

Eyes of an arrogant, but gentle stranger
eyes I once knew so well
        why is the night so still?

Arms I remember
rainbow that died
        thunder that crashed on a hill

Smile of a proud and an intimate stranger
thoughts I can clearly hear
bringing familiar pain
dream half-forgotten
music that echoes
        why did it start to rain?

"Come on, let's go—don't be so slow"

        (did someone say Alsace Lorraine?)

"Not me. You'd better hurry if you don't want to miss
        your plane"

Butterfly Will Get Her Revenge

(IF SHE KNOWS HER ASTROLOGY)

Let's face it
Lt. Pinkerton was a Gemini

    And if he were real, instead of fictional

it would serve him right
to reincarnate
one fine day
as a Virgo or a Pisces
with an afflicted Venus

        and get mixed up
        with Butterfly again
        who, hopefully
        would reincarnate
        as a Scorpio
        with the Moon in Scorpio
        and Venus in Scorpio
        and a Scorpio Ascendant
        and Mars in Aries

That would teach him a karmic lesson or two!

Pass the Peace Pipe

(THE CAPITULATION OF A CARDINAL SIGN)

You want to call the shots?
All right, jump on your horse
and I'll walk three respectful steps behind
like a proper squaw

You decide the course and by-ways
our stream of madness shall run
    how it bends and wanders
and where and when it flows
into the land-of-the-singing-waters

I'll chew my moccasins and string my wampum
in the pale, new moon, beside my wickiup
and wait for your bird call, tom-tom beat or smoke puff

but remember, brave Chief Rain-in-the-Heart
while you lead us down this sun–danced warpath
of pride and passion, truth and lie
the spirits of the wind and stars are watching
and it's Manitou who calls the final shots
    not you or I

Sun in Earth—Moon in Air or Water

I can't write you love songs that make you cry
or understand your fascination for things that fly
I wear black a lot
because I look awful in red

> but I'll butter your bread and make up your bed
> with sheets that have hung in the sun

I won't be the first woman to land on the moon

> (I don't even like to travel to Boston
> unless there's a good, solid reason for the trip)

but I'll walk with you
halfway up the hill
feed you vegetable soup when you're feeling ill
and I never forget to take the Pill
I'm not the careless or flighty type

> I'm not new and exciting, like I was when we met
> I always catch cold when my feet get wet
> and then my nose turns pink

But I'll never leave curlers in the bathroom sink
or chatter
when you're looking for the missing link to your latest dream

> You haven't said "I love you" since we ordered
>   champagne from that funny French waiter
> but tonight you said "I need you"
>   just before you fell asleep, a little later

Afterwards I lay awake
in the sticky heat that promised a storm
till finally I slipped out of bed around three

to sit in your chair awhile
and think about you and me

      Then I remembered a verse I read
      when you were away so long last fall
      I tore the page out of a library book
      which isn't like me at all

It said
   (at least the lines that mattered)
"Being needed is as good as being loved
sometimes—even better"

So I darned the hole in your favorite green sweater
put a stamp on your mother's letter
turned out the light and locked the door
      (I thought I had locked it before
      but I hadn't)

When I lay down beside you again
I felt the slow, steady beat of your heart
as you reached out to touch me, half-dreaming
and at last, it started to rain

      But, darling, my name isn't Laura
      It's Jane . . .

Maybe I'll make pancakes for breakfast
with those little sausages you like

      I'll call him in the morning
         after you've gone into town

      Now, where did I write his number down?

And—
what should I say?

> "I'm kind of at loose ends, if you want to stop
> by today?"

> Yes, that sounds casual enough

Delinquent Bread and Butter Letter
Mailed under a Full Moon

When I was young and thoughtless
my grandmother used to say
that a well-bred person
always writes a grateful line or two
after being a guest in someone's home
or the recipient of some smaller kindness

> as she tried to smooth the rough and splintered edges
> of a fiery Mars nature, molded carelessly
> > near Albuquerque
> for April's impulsive spring

I guess it did some good
Since then, I've dutifully sent gratuity notes
to friends and strangers
even a couple of times
to enemies

> But today, from the club car of the Metroliner
> I saw a meadow, washed silvery clean
> by sheets of early morning fog

and suddenly, I remembered
that I forgot
to thank you
for certain, private smiles
and other, odd, assorted gifts

for the room
where we almost loved
that smelled of pine and rainy forests

> for Indians and ships and astral trips
> celebrations of Guy Fawkes Day

things that died—and were born again
on the 26th of May
happy jet flights through western skies
and sad, Japanese Butterflys

for teaching me
how closely related
passion and patience can be

for helping me through my homework
in the kind of math
where one and one
make three

and all those lovely colors

snow white truth on coral beaches
blue Ave Marias
and pink champagne
green, talking plants
deep, red sunsets
purple arguments
a piece of possible gold
grey photographs of yesterday
and the lilac shades
of freedom from the fear of growing old

I'll write tonight

Dear You
Thanks for giving me an occasional rainbow
and how did you know
it was exactly what I needed?

A Valentine for Leo, with Love

Once upon a time
there was this awfully ferocious Lion
with a beautiful mane of long, curly hair

      who maybe was not always right
      though God knows he was never wrong

He didn't roar often, but when he did
the stars hid behind the clouds
and every animal in the jungle shivered and shook
not only with fear
but in awe of the King's majestic dignity

      Once on a hot, muggy night
      after a dry, dusty day
      when everyone's adrenalin was acting up

all the animals decided to fight each other to the death
for no special reason
at least, none that even the elephants can remember

      So of course they had to have a leader
      who was courageous
      and with it
      and confident and clever and conceited
      and all that

Shrewdly assessing the Lion's compassion for the weak
they picked a perfect patsy as a messenger
      a tiny, gentle, one-eyed monkey
      whose tail had been blasted off
      by some brave and fearless sportsmen
and whose fickle wife had run off with a swinging Cheetah

After a top secret briefing by a flat-headed cobra and an owl
this sad-faced loner was sent to rap with the King
          of the jungle
and discuss the animals' bloody proposition

      The monkey told the Lion
      he could lead either side he chose
      as long as neither was deprived of a fair share
         of killings
      (or he could fight on both sides if he liked
      though that would take some diplomatic hustling)

Lying languidly in his scented hammock
this awfully ferocious Lion with the beautiful mane
          of long, curly hair

listened carefully to the slick pitch
of the one-eyed, tailless, wifeless monkey
privately deciding
he'd never buy a used car from him for obvious reasons

      then he yawned a luxurious Leonine yawn and said

        "Tell them to cool it, Man
        Hell no—I won't go"

When the animals heard the Lion's answer
they were absolutely knocked out
The proud, royal King of their jungle a coward?

      It stung, to say the least

They voted to kill him immediately, of course

      if not sooner

but there was a law against that
you see, the war hadn't officially been declared yet
and timing is everything, even in jungle society
   Like—
   if you're going to mess around with taking lives
   you've got to play by the rules

So they decided, instead
to lock him up
for 33 years and 3 days

     in the cave where Tarzan used to keep
      Maureen O'Sullivan

      and do you know what happened?

       He escaped!

     because all the animals were afraid to stand guard

      not one of them was as strong as the Lion

       not a single one

Fragile Neptune Doesn't Groove
with Earth Signs

I go now to seek a Prince
in a secret part of the forest
who waits for me in shivering quiet
his step too light to bruise the earth
who walks on moonlight beside a singing waterfall

I go now to seek a Prince
to call him through the midnight sky
so we might fly away to search for ancient druids
hiding in the woods below the violet hills out there

My heart will fill with rich and gentle velvet
and with peace
as we submit to careless passionate showers
of blending
to laugh and sigh and weep—to know each other
under blankets woven loosely
of twilight's private world

I go now to seek a Prince

    I find a mortal man
    who wears a frown
    just above the horn-rimmed glasses on his nose
    whose firmly locked intentions close out the songs of joy
    whose clothes hang neatly in a closet of exact dimensions
    waiting for the morning's measured schedule

He's tired by nine
a glass of wine brings dreamless, sterile sleep
the clock his unrelenting ruler
his habits screwed in tight

He greets me cold
with disapproving gaze and tone
    "It's late"
I stand accused and guilty

Poor blind, chained soul
still young in years, though aging swiftly in the heart
he knows not yet how late it really is

Libra in Love

Giving that man a job and a reason to live
in spite of what everyone said
was kind

    I like you

Setting that bird's broken wing
and teaching him how to fly again
near the foot of that ancient tree
was beautiful

    I love you

Spending your precious moments lighting the angles
and arranging the pose of a strange nude
is crude

    I hate you

Will you please send back my friendship ring
and take your foot off my scales?

Sting of the Scorpion

Your icy voice put out the stars
it cracked my heart and broke it in splinters
your tone as cold as Colorado winters

        But I promise to soon forget
        the contract we almost made
        You'll feel the swift response of an equal
        as the dream begins to fade

I'll drown you in pseudo-kindness
and a casual, friendly glance
I can almost imagine your blindness
        as I watch and wait for the chance
        to suddenly—cruelly—make you know
        how easy it was to let you go

Astrology Lesson

"Mars is the ruler of Aries"
   "*Nothing* rules Aries"
"Mars is the ruler of the first house"
   "*That's* better"

Jupiter Approaching the Midheaven

Why did we stop in that shabby little bar
last Friday
after our long, weary walk to nowhere?

> Was it a chance to talk among strangers
> away from the dangers of being alone
> with our unspoken need to atone
>   for something unknown?

The first thing I saw was a sign, in the mirror

ICE COLD BEER

that seemed to spell backwards, through distorted reflection

ICE COLD FEAR

Funny thought to get caught in my head
but all I said was, "It's chilly in here
I should have brought my sweater"

> Suddenly, I was hungry
>   (this time, for food)
> so I asked for a cheeseburger
> with cheese on both sides

It was quite a jar to the gregarious fellow behind the bar
He really lost his cool
Remember the look on his face?

> "Now how in the hell can my cook do that
> without the cheese stickin' all over his griddle?
> In fourteen years as a bartender
> I never had nobody
> want cheese on both sides"

"You never met nobody like this before"
you told him

as he mumbled "Amen"

When several minutes crawled by
and we still hadn't started to talk
I began to pray
we'd find a way to end the awkward silence

It's always like that . . .

After a while, my beer tasted flat
and I drank a sip of yours
to see
if it was the beer
or me

Then you asked that blasphemous question

"What are you doing, taking holy communion?"

Well, since communion and confession go together
I guess I'd better tell you
the stale taste of my beer was an excuse
All right, it was a lie
I just wanted to drink from your glass
and I swear on my life I don't know why

Finally the waiter brought over my order
with cheese on both sides
bursting with pride at his cook's baptism
in gourmet dishes

"Well, whatta ya know, he made it—
and he didn't get none on his griddle!"

It was such a happy moment, I almost made
    three wishes
like I used to do
when I saw a white horse, from a car
or the first evening star
back home

Strange, how the smallest things sometimes suffice
to break the ice of the lonely distance between us

    We grinned at each other then
    and started to talk at last
    and stayed so late, over a few more beers
    we missed our date with a couple of friends
    we hadn't seen for years

When we remembered the time, you paid the bill
and left some change on the plate

    But
    did you notice the light through the stained
        glass window?
        (stained by tobacco and years of grime)
    and the freckled lad playing the pinball
    with a smile like an altar boy?

There was kind of an aura
around that place we found
on our Good Friday search
    for God
It reminded me of a church
    isn't that odd?

Song of the Ram

Spring may surprise me this year

I might actually literally find myself
on the Champs Élysées
with nothing to do but make love with you
in an attic room overlooking the Seine
or lying on the grass in the Bois de Boulogne

and suddenly, I'll notice it's April

Or I could just as easily wake up in the Highlands
drenched in an uncanny, golden glow
mingled with the spray of a fine Scottish mist
like the one I ran through
in a flash of déjà vu
one day at an airport in the mountains

I'll spend lazy hours
shopping for a haunted old castle to live in
since I just won the Pulitzer prize
You'll be reading to me from Robert Burns
under Edinburgh skies

and suddenly, I'll remember it's April

I might fly down the aisle
of a wildflower church in the Alps
ringing its bells for joy

and it's possible I'll win the Irish Sweepstakes
the same day my musical opens on Broadway
with floodlights and stars
like a gigantic Mike Todd production

or be born again—singing
in some little cemetery
taking its time
out west

      Spring owes me something

So far, she's pulled off a few splendid sparklers
a fat, rosy angel who stayed for awhile
      a make-believe tree house
and once, a shiny gold ring

but not a real Block Buster Sky Rocket miracle
like she always promised

      Maybe this year, unexpectedly

Underexposed Negative of Saturn

He's an artist who lives near Big Sur, by the ocean
no kin of blood—or heart—to me
yet I found myself trembling
and shudder now
remembering our twilight conversation

> "I don't believe in reincarnation," he smiled
> "except in the most general way
> but let me tell you what happened
> one August day
> in Victor, Colorado . . .
> Look—here's a picture I took
> for no reason I can logically explain
> just a sign painted on a window
> WELCOME TO THE CITY OF GOLD MINES"

> *(Welcome—familiar stranger*
> *but beware*
> *beware of what danger?)*

His words tumbled out, first halting, then fast
like a broken, remembered refrain from the past
I hear it still—and will I always?

> "Victor, Colorado—elevation ten thousand feet
> at that height, you hardly feel the heat of summer
> I was obsessed by an urgent need
> to photograph the scene
> as if the camera eye could find
> what lay behind the proud and quiet privacy
> of that little mining town
> with buildings falling down
> like London bridges . . .
> in Wales, I thought
> the miners dig for coal, not gold

and they grow old before their time
strange recollection . . .
what could an island across the sea
have to do with Colorado—or with me?
Here are some more shots I brought back
black, lusterless rocks
piled around broken old mine shafts
why should their cold, misshapen heaps
loom so eloquent, yet ominous
against the sky?"

I watched him sigh
a faint, beginning horror
scratching on the consciousness
denied admittance

> "And here's a picture of a haunted house
> it's odd, but I was sure I had seen it before
> gingerbread trim—bay windows—double door"

> > *(and something more
> > something more. . . .)*

> "Then this—another mine
> deserted—see?
> with the figures 1-2-3 painted on the side"

As he stared at me, I closed my eyes
What secrets could those numbers hide
to strike the faint and shrouded echoes of sobbing
in my breast?

> "The sea was far away
> from where, then, did I hear the sound of
>   crashing waves
> and why the strangling sensation of drowning
> tightening in my chest?

an eerie and unlikely dream for August, Leo's month
A few miles further on I came upon a graveyard
dull, lifeless cemetery clay, dusty and choking
permeated with the aura of unearthly stillness
surrounding the bodies buried just below
where tall, lonely trees, centuries old
stood loyal vigil over the dead
an inexpressibly sad curve to their posture
What did I seek?
The anguished shriek of a single bird
tore across the silence
bringing a tentative flash of awareness
quickly absorbed in the thin, dry mountain air
only a beat removed from memory . . ."

>   *(Memory of what?*
>   *From where?)*

"As I walked on slowly, hesitating
I heard the far-off whistle of a train
and cursed the subtle, unsuspected madness
in my brain
that led me on this senseless search
of a town with a red brick Baptist church
hiding grey, forgotten ghosts inside . . ."

>   *(and one Welshman with his bride?*
>   *Déjà vu—déjà vu)*

From somewhere . . .
did he hear it too?
soft chords of organ music drifted through
then broke in strange discordant patterns

>   "Christ! What kind of man
>   could live a lifetime
>   in that god-forsaken place?"

An unexpected trace of anger lit his face
and spilled into the empty space between us
till I could see him lost near distant hills
I knew as well as he
where some once thought the streets were paved with gold
"Solid gold, I tell you, Tom!"
Did someone speak across the bleak, forbidding landscape
his words had stirred?
No, the only voice was his
as the night grew dark with unspoken recognition
of remembered wrath

   "Although I swear I've never trod that path
   I seemed to be compelled
   to return once more
   and explore the cemetery
   driven by an intangible anticipation of discovery. . . .
   This time
   I noticed weeds, growing rampant and wild
   around a slanting headstone
   bleached, faded monument
   to love and life
   RESTING HERE: BELOVED WIFE"

      (of whom?)

   "The name had been obscured
         by sun and pounding rain
   but someone, once, had grieved for her, I knew
   because I felt a deep, sharp stab of pain
   a kind of—what do they call it—déjà vu?"

      Yes, déjà vu
      Snap a shot of soldiers now
      marching off to hell

Over there—over there
a marker fell
and lies in wait

"Later, after I had photographed some
    soldiers' graves
fifty some odd yards away . . ."

How had I known
what he was going to say?

"Wandering aimless, mind numb and hypnotized
by the sameness of the scenery
I almost fell into a deep ravine
that stretched before me, just ahead
empty, yawning abyss—
and at my feet—what's this? I said
humble object over which to stumble
a marker, made of wood, not stone
from a nearby grave, now long neglected and alone
so I propped it up against a fence post in the grass
interesting shot—why not?
but my clammy fingers fumbled on the shutter
as a rumble shook the air
summer thunder, common there, I guess
though it made me wonder, I must confess
about that simple, unpretentious marker
waiting for the curious or the clumsy
lettered lovingly with a steady hand
words raised in relief
from three score years or so
of winter's ice and snow
three infant's names 1-2-3
died too soon. . . ."

(Yes, died too soon, too soon, too soon)

"By late afternoon
the film was nearly gone
the sun was spreading gold across the west
Skip the rest, I thought
what does all this mean to me?
but then—was that a voice I heard—a sigh?
'Now Tom, why run away?
women don't always mean what they say'
the thin, electric Colorado air
plays illusionary tricks upon the mind—
            was that a cry?
'Lad, what if she should die?'

When I picked up the marker
it burned my hand
an imaginary reaction
for the fleeting fraction of a timeless moment—
but I decided to take it home with me
why let it lay unnoticed
on the ground?
My mind was full of questions, each unanswered
Was that a flash of lightning?
      the sky is clear
Whose heart was that I just heard break?
am I trespassing here?"

He paused, confused

"I still don't understand
why I brought back a tombstone for a souvenir"

Return to the present
uncertain
behind the curtain of nameless fear

"Would you like to see it?"

As he handed me the marker
I could feel a scalding tear
my soul was chilled
though wide awake
I knew too well I must not tell
whose heart it was that he heard break
in Victor, Colorado

Study Your Own Ephemeris

Look, just because I'm an astrologer
that doesn't mean I know *everything*
              (though I thank you for the compliment)

When you wondered why
we wrote all that music together
and fought over every single note
I told you that your progressed Mars
was opposing my natal Mercury

              When you asked me what made it rain
              at exactly the moment you first kissed me
              standing on that village street
              I told you the Moon was in a water sign
              trining both our Suns

Then you wanted to know
why we saw a rainbow through the snow
one morning in the cemetery
so I explained that Neptune was in Scorpio
sextile Jupiter in Pisces

Last night you had a new question

              "What's going to happen between us?"

Well, I'll tell you this much
Very soon now
Pluto will conjunct your Venus

              I've known it since the beginning
              Study your Ephemeris, darling

The Puzzlement of 28 IF

Alas and alack, alas and alack, what have we here?
Kiss a red carnation black—with one blue tear
Double, double, time-track trouble
pick a strawberry four-leaf clover
play it backwards, play it over

> Don't cry, little lass, don't cry
> he's still alive—he didn't die
> he's writing songs for three blind mice
> and the farmer's wife

did you ever hear such a tale in your life?

> Step aside, girl, and let him pass
> walkin' barefoot through the grass
> and Hey, Hey, Hey! Isn't it groovy, like
>   Christmas Day?
> he's still around in London town
> with the farmer's wife and three blind mice

Play it backwards, listen twice, three blind mice
then thank a song of sixpence if you're bright enough to see
bright enough to see . . .

> and Paul

Oh, Paul, dear Paul, the gentle one
>   (see how they run—see how they run?)
sing your Noel songs still sweetly

> But do take care now, won't you Luv?
> when they shove up close to hear you
> please take caution and beware
> of those flash bulbs poppin' near you

for 'tis written on an ancient scroll
that the eyes are the windows of the soul

> See how they run
> after Paul, the gentle one?
> the eyes, ah yes! the eyes
> are the windows of the soul

Sagittarian Wife's Lament

I've only had one husband
but he had two heads

    He was a Gemini
and my astrologer warned me that we were square
       to each other
or something—

    Boy! You can say that again!

Before he broke the news, he killed a quart of booze
all by himself
(He found the bottle on the shelf behind the china piggy bank
where I should have known better than to hide it)

    But in spite of all that rye
    he didn't even slur his words when he said goodbye
    or seem to be grieving
    He sounded like Basil Rathbone
    "So long, dear Duchess, I'm leaving"

I said "Good Riddance"
and I meant it
who needs all those charming lies?

    (he had such gentle, dark brown eyes)

So he took his LP of Der Rosenkavelier
the shells we gathered last summer at the Pier
his golf clubs—his copy of Roget's Thesaurus
and split

    That was last night

Today I was cleaning the garbage out of his desk
    (I don't know why)
and I came across this verse he wrote

    He was probably on a vodka high
    I mean he must have been really smashed
    as drunk as a skunk
    to write that kind of junk
    It doesn't even rhyme
    Just listen

"Into the dream you came
and across the soft carpet of my reverie you walked
with hobnail boots"

Lecture to a Lion Tuned In to Uranus

Now, see here
you can't just go around
expecting everybody to be concerned
about the dangers of the oil depletion allowance
and the disappearance of plankton

  or thinking that everyone understands
why Emil White built his own tree house in the woods
or why Henry Miller paints sweet and sour, like he writes
    (maybe because he lived in the Orient
    in another life)

Not everyone has heard about Edgar Cayce and his trances
or Cleve Backster's polygraphs and plants

Sometimes you have to come down from the lighthouse
and play with the sandpipers
  skipping and staggering on the beach
if you want them to eat the crumbs of eternity
you've stored up to feed them
now that winter is coming to the world

My God, some people still go to Roseland Ballroom
and dance all night
to "One O'Clock Jump" and "Stella By Starlight"

  or save up for one of those group vacations in Hawaii
  and bring home color Polaroids
  of hula girls hanging leis around their necks

or squeeze into a nightclub
where they charge $20 to use the tablecloth
and wait in line outside, afterwards
for hours
to get Engelbert Humperdinck's autograph

Saturn Seen from Gesthemene in Late December

Would you hear them just as clearly ring
if St. Michael's bells could not swing free
because the tower long ago was locked
            or would your spring be robbed
            of every promise?

Would you still see the garden's blazing glory
if sunset never told its sensual story
but hid behind the shadowed sorrow of the past
            or would Mori's castle crumble then, at last?

Can a barren winter bring the balm you seek
when its virgin snowflakes only kiss your cheek
then melt in tears?

Will you reach beyond these frozen midnight fears
heaven has refused to bless
with the peace that April rains release
        or will the bright and hopeful song you sing
        soon cease?

Will I still find you here
as near
if you should guess
what loneliness cannot confess
while there are seven mountains yet to climb?

            Yes
        until the end of time

Uranus—Neptune—Pluto— and Reincarnation

I'd like to give the world a Christmas present
before I have to go

a pair of glasses
            with multiple lens
to help the eyes see long ago
            then you would know
the reason for the music

12th House Affliction

I must go now

       don't hold me with your eyes
       and reach your heart across the room like that

          or my own will break

       Love you?
       Of course I love you
       that's why I have to go, before you know

          how much

Tomorrow, I'll be stronger
and we'll walk up to the Garden of the Gods again
and look for Indian arrowheads

          for luck

Echo of Mars Unaroused

You see?
I am still me

      The secret place inside
      where my heart will always hide
      from the withering clutch of too much need
      has not been reached

I remain myself
with courage still to face the sun

      It's not a hollow victory I've won
         to still be me

Why should I grieve?
My dreams are made of sterner stuff
and Spring will be here soon enough . . .